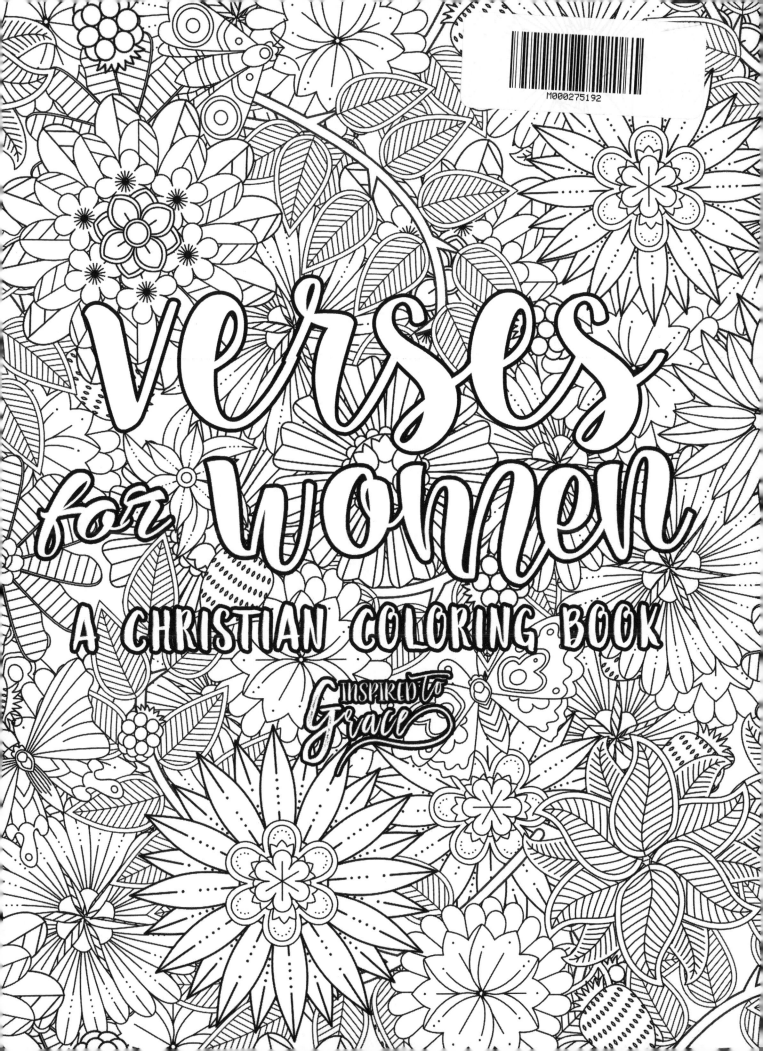

FREE DOWNLOAD

Yahweh is a compassionate **and gracious** God, → slow to anger ← **and rich** in faithful **love and truth.** Exodus 34:6

OUR SOUL **WAITS FOR THE LORD** PSALM 33:20

BLESSED ARE THE peacemakers MATTHEW 5:9

www.inspiredtograce.com/women

YOUR DOWNLOAD CODE: WN7923

@inspiredtograce

Inspired to Grace

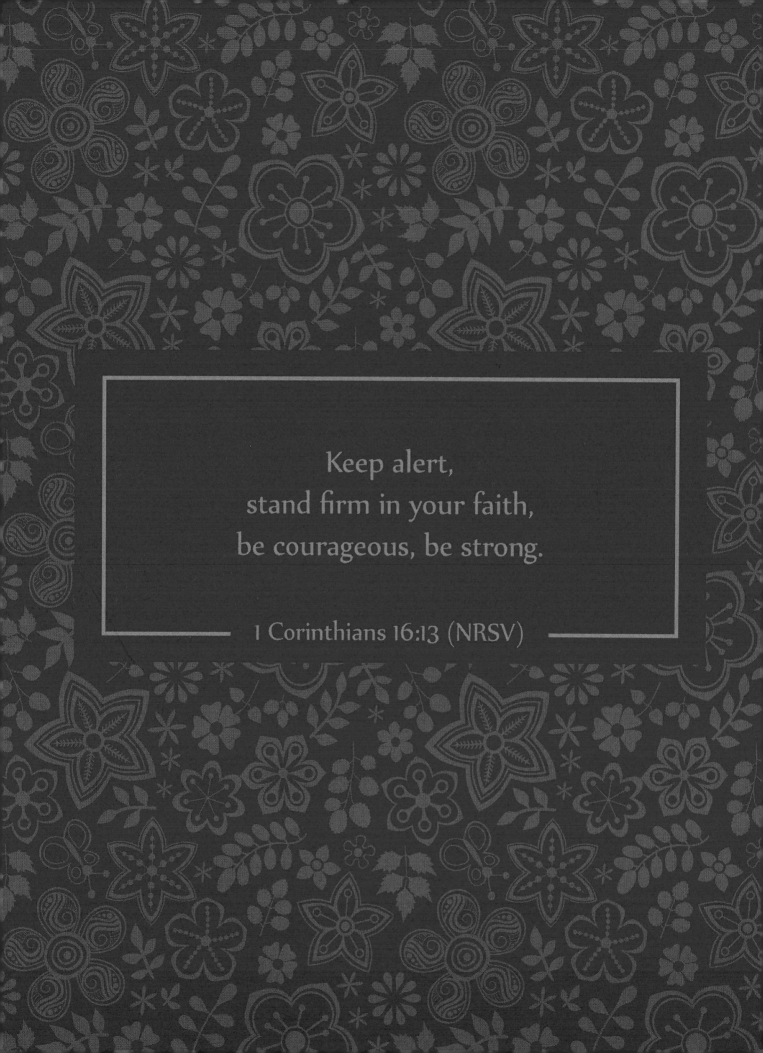

Keep alert,
stand firm in your faith,
be courageous, be strong.

1 Corinthians 16:13 (NRSV)

The end of all things is near. Therefore be alert and of sober mind so that you may pray. Above all, love each other deeply, because love covers over a multitude of sins. Offer hospitality to one another without grumbling. Each of you should use whatever gift you have received to serve others, as faithful stewards of God's grace in its various forms.

1 Peter 4:7-10 (NIV)

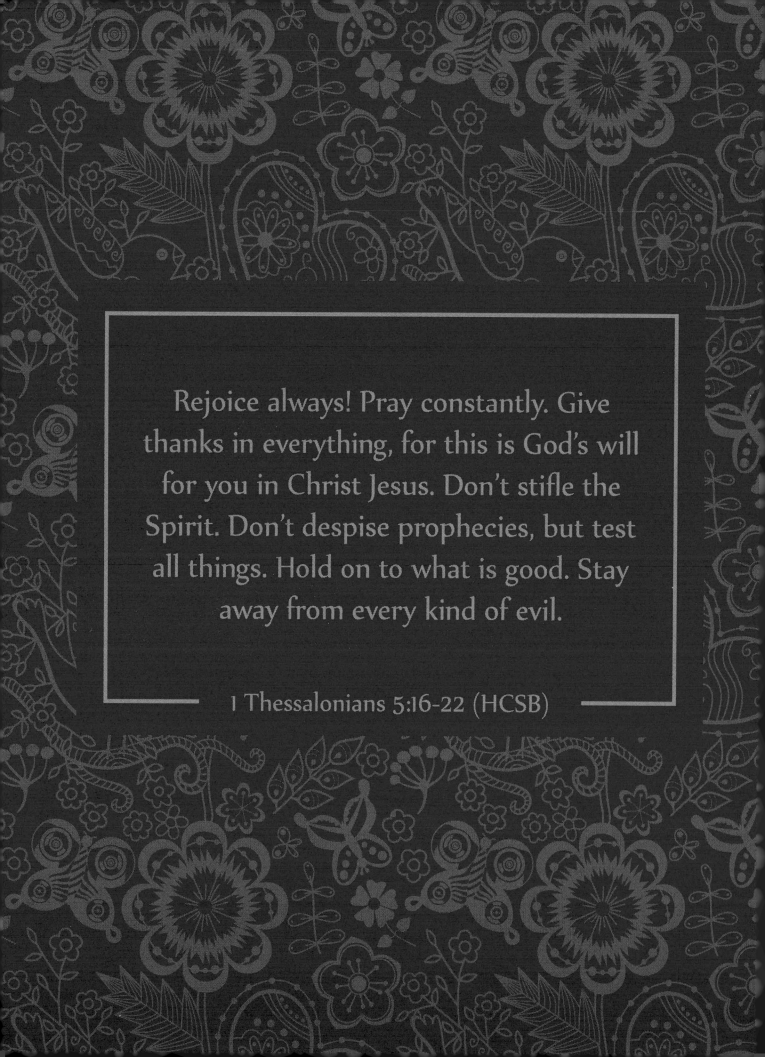

Rejoice always! Pray constantly. Give thanks in everything, for this is God's will for you in Christ Jesus. Don't stifle the Spirit. Don't despise prophecies, but test all things. Hold on to what is good. Stay away from every kind of evil.

1 Thessalonians 5:16-22 (HCSB)

Then Moses went out and spoke these words to all Israel: "I am now a hundred and twenty years old and I am no longer able to lead you. The Lord has said to me, 'You shall not cross the Jordan.' The Lord your God himself will cross over ahead of you. He will destroy these nations before you, and you will take possession of their land. Joshua also will cross over ahead of you, as the Lord said. And the Lord will do to them what he did to Sihon and Og, the kings of the Amorites, whom he destroyed along with their land. The Lord will deliver them to you, and you must do to them all that I have commanded you. Be strong and courageous. Do not be afraid or terrified because of them, for the Lord your God goes with you; he will never leave you nor forsake you."

Deuteronomy 31:1-6 (NIV)

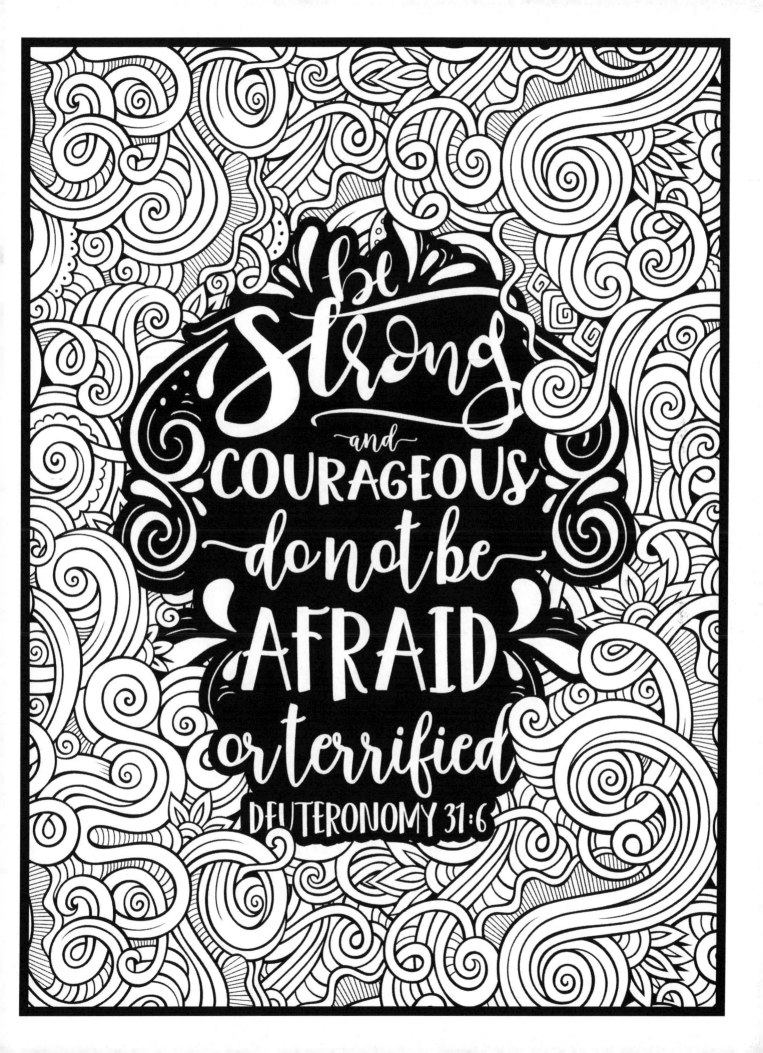

Glory in his holy name; let the hearts of those who seek the Lord rejoice. Seek the Lord and his strength, seek his presence continually.

1 Chronicles 16:10-11 (NRSV)

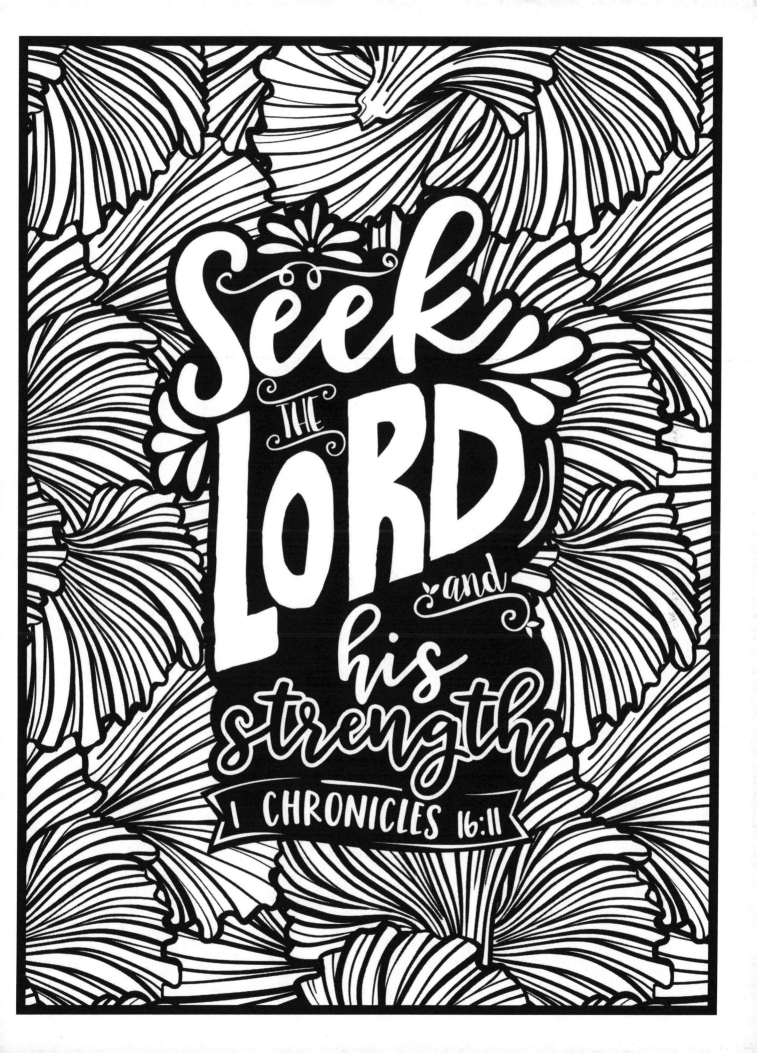

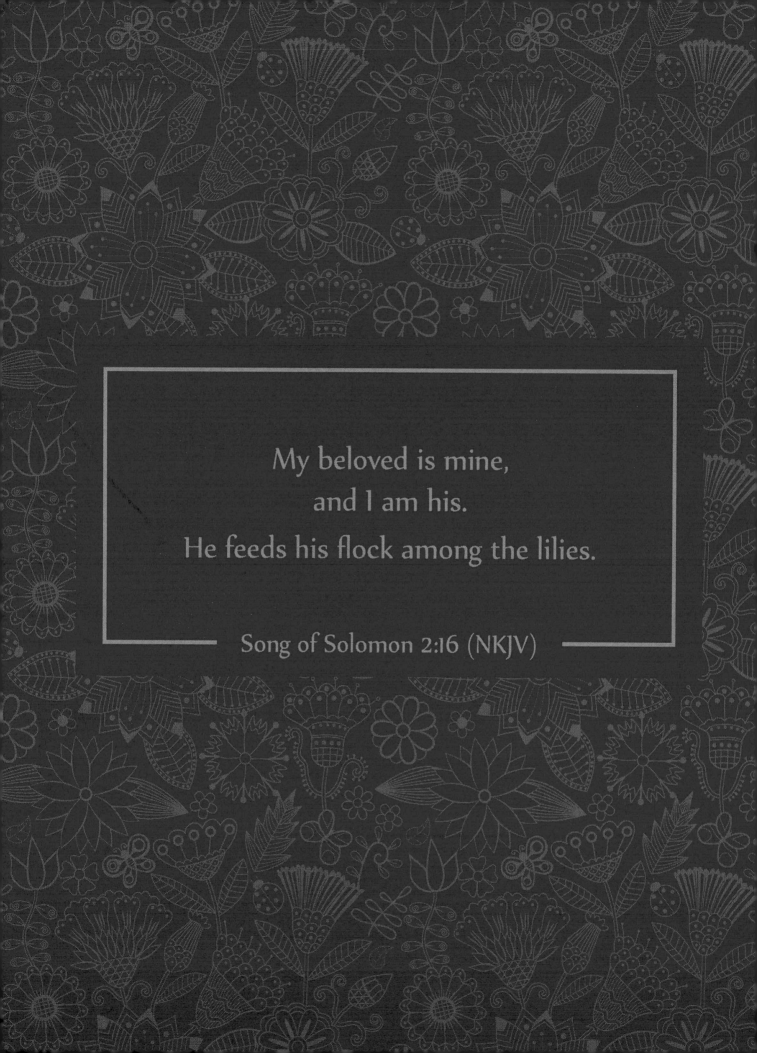

My beloved is mine,
and I am his.
He feeds his flock among the lilies.

Song of Solomon 2:16 (NKJV)

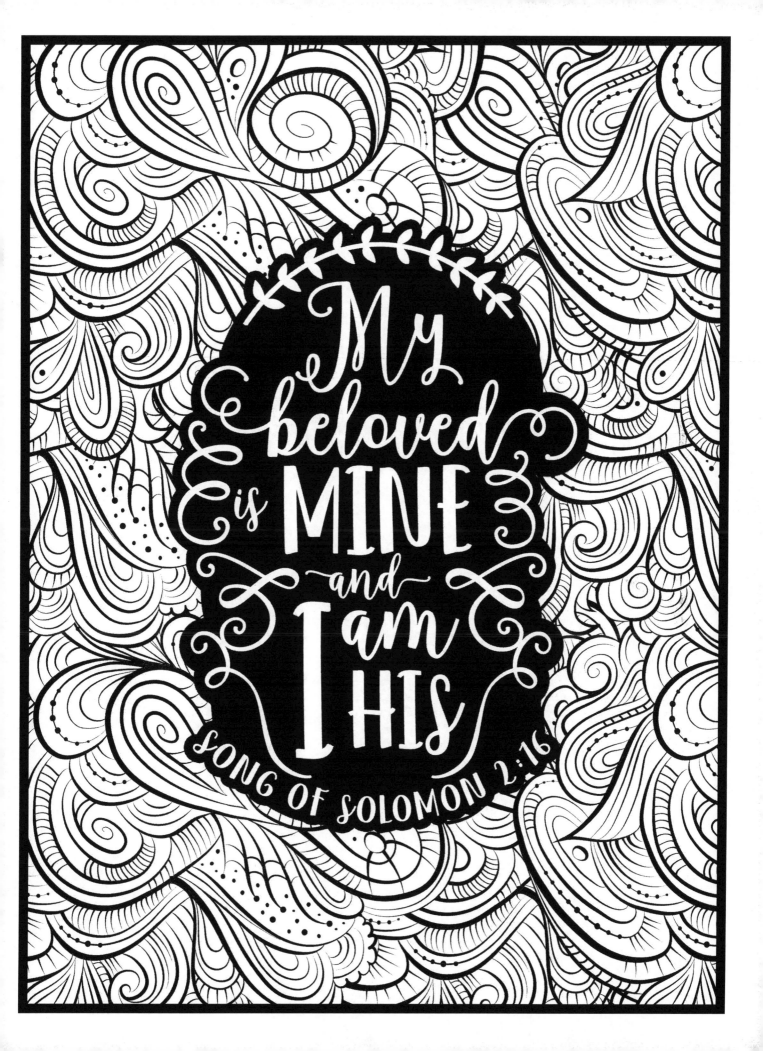

What profit has the worker from that in which he labors? I have seen the God-given task with which the sons of men are to be occupied. He has made everything beautiful in its time. Also he has put eternity in their hearts, except that no one can find out the work that God does from beginning to end.

Ecclesiastes 3:9-11 (NKJV)

Then the Lord passed in front of him
and proclaimed: Yahweh – Yahweh is
a compassionate and gracious God,
slow to anger and rich in faithful love
and truth, maintaining faithful love
to a thousand generations, forgiving
wrongdoing, rebellion, and sin. But he
will not leave the guilty unpunished,
bringing the consequences of the
fathers' wrongdoing on the children and
grandchildren to the third and fourth
generation.

Exodus 34:6-7 (HCSB)

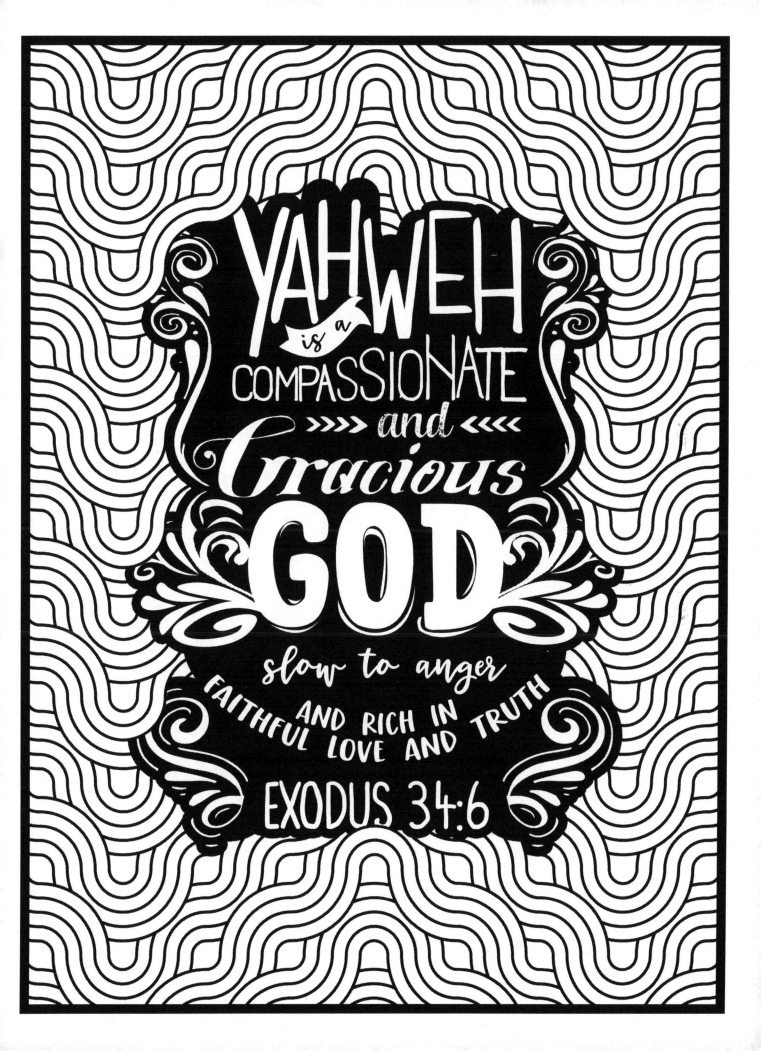

A voice was saying, "Cry out!"
Another said, "What should I cry out?"
"All humanity is grass, and all its
goodness is like the flower of the field.
The grass withers, the flowers fade when
the breath of the Lord blows on them;
indeed, the people are grass. The grass
withers, the flowers fade, but the word
of our God remains forever.

Isaiah 40:6-8 (HCSB)

The grass withers, the flowers fade, but the word of our God remains forever

ISAIAH 40:8

The Lord appeared to us in the past, saying: "I have loved you with an everlasting love; I have drawn you with unfailing kindness. I will build you up again, and you, Virgin Israel, will be rebuilt. Again you will take up your timbrels and go out to dance with the joyful. Again you will plant vineyards on the hills of Samaria; the farmers will plant them and enjoy their fruit. There will be a day when watchmen cry out on the hills of Ephraim, 'Come, let us go up to Zion, to the Lord our God.'"

Jeremiah 31:3-6 (NIV)

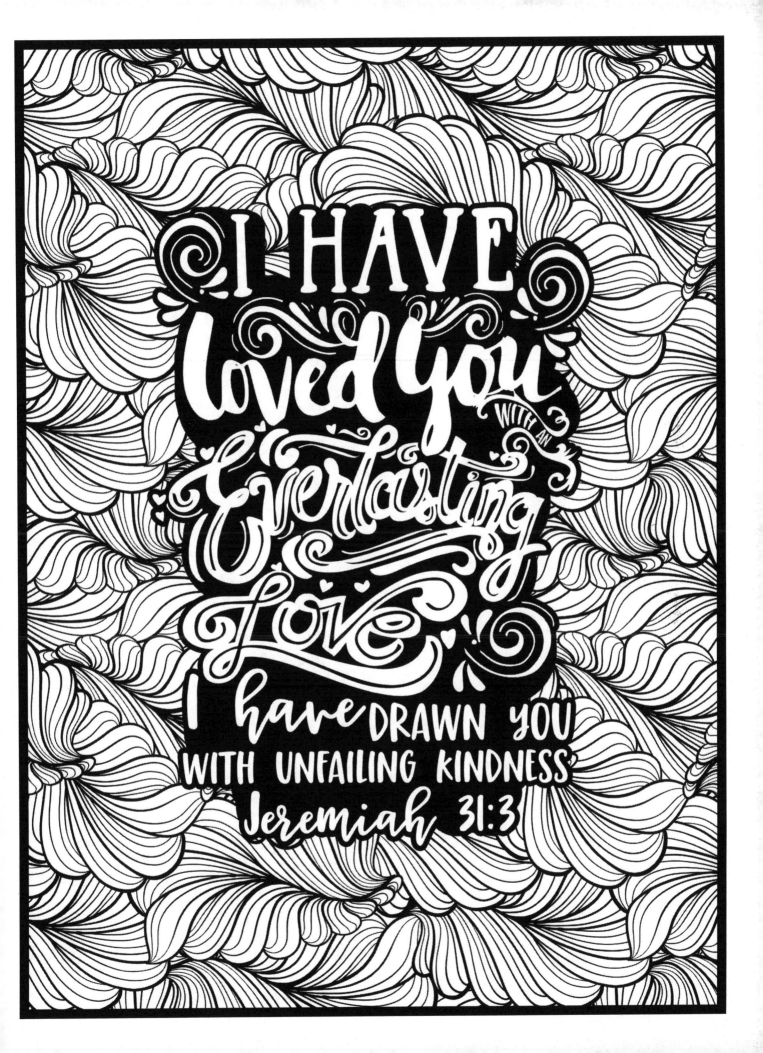

Blessed are the peacemakers: for they shall be called the children of God. Blessed are they which are persecuted for righteousness' sake: for theirs is the kingdom of heaven.

Matthew 5:9-10 (KJV)

A wife of noble character who can find? She is worth far more than rubies. Her husband has full confidence in her and lacks nothing of value. She brings him good, not harm, all the days of her life.

Proverbs 31:10-12 (NIV)

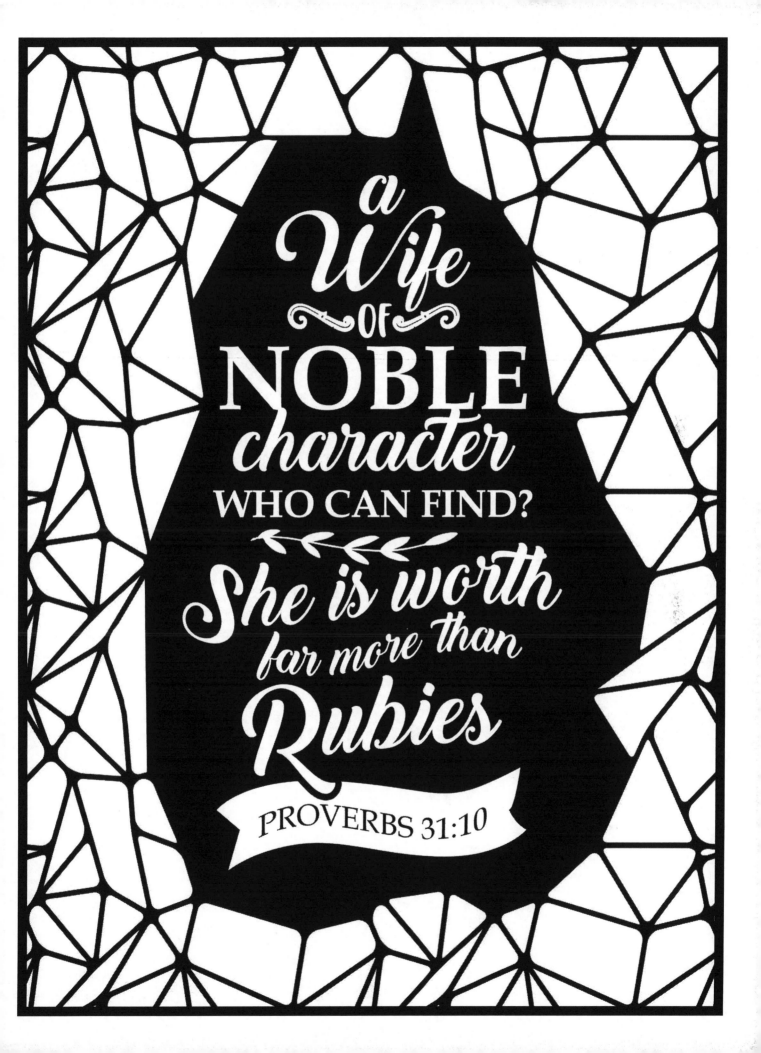

Good comes to those who lend money
generously and conduct their business
fairly. Such people will not be overcome
by evil. Those who are righteous will be
long remembered. They do not fear bad
news; they confidently trust the Lord
to care for them. They are confident
and fearless and can face their foes
triumphantly.

Psalm 112:5-8 (NLT)

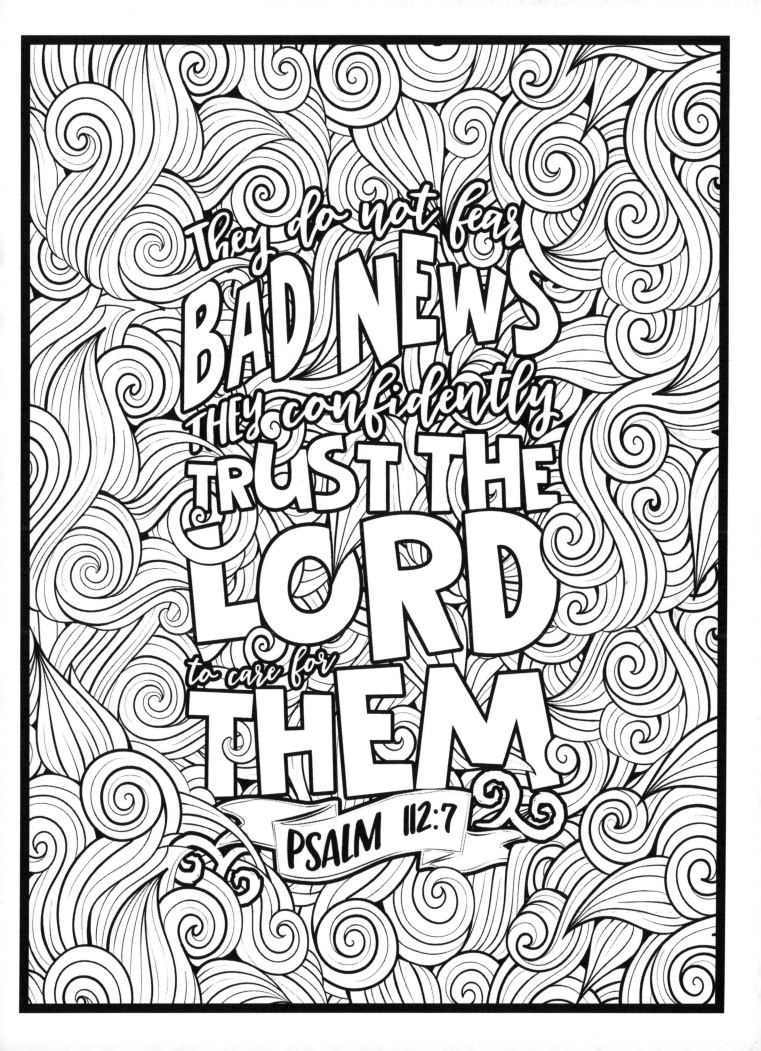

Give thanks to the Lord,
for he is good;
his love endures forever.

Psalm 107:1 (NIV)

What then are we to say about these things? If God is for us, who is against us? He who did not withhold his own Son, but gave him up for all of us, will he not with him also give us everything else? Who will bring any charge against God's elect? It is God who justifies. Who is to condemn? It is Christ Jesus, who died, yes, who was raised, who is at the right hand of God, who indeed intercedes for us.

Romans 8:31-34 (NRSV)

How beautiful you are,
my darling, how beautiful!
Your eyes are like doves.

Song of Solomon 1:15 (NLT)

How beautiful you are, my darling! Oh, how beautiful! Your eyes behind your veil are doves. Your hair is like a flock of goats descending from the hills of Gilead. Your teeth are like a flock of sheep just shorn, coming up from the washing. Each has its twin; not one of them is alone.

Song of Solomon 4:1-2 (NIV)

You are altogether beautiful, my love; there is no flaw in you. Come with me from Lebanon, my bride; come with me from Lebanon. Depart from the peak of Amana, from the peak of Senir and Hermon, from the dens of lions, from the mountains of leopards.

Song of Solomon 4:7-8 (NRSV)

Have you never heard? Have you never understood? The Lord is the everlasting God, the Creator of all the earth. He never grows weak or weary. No one can measure the depths of his understanding. He gives power to the weak and strength to the powerless.

Isaiah 40:28-29 (NLT)

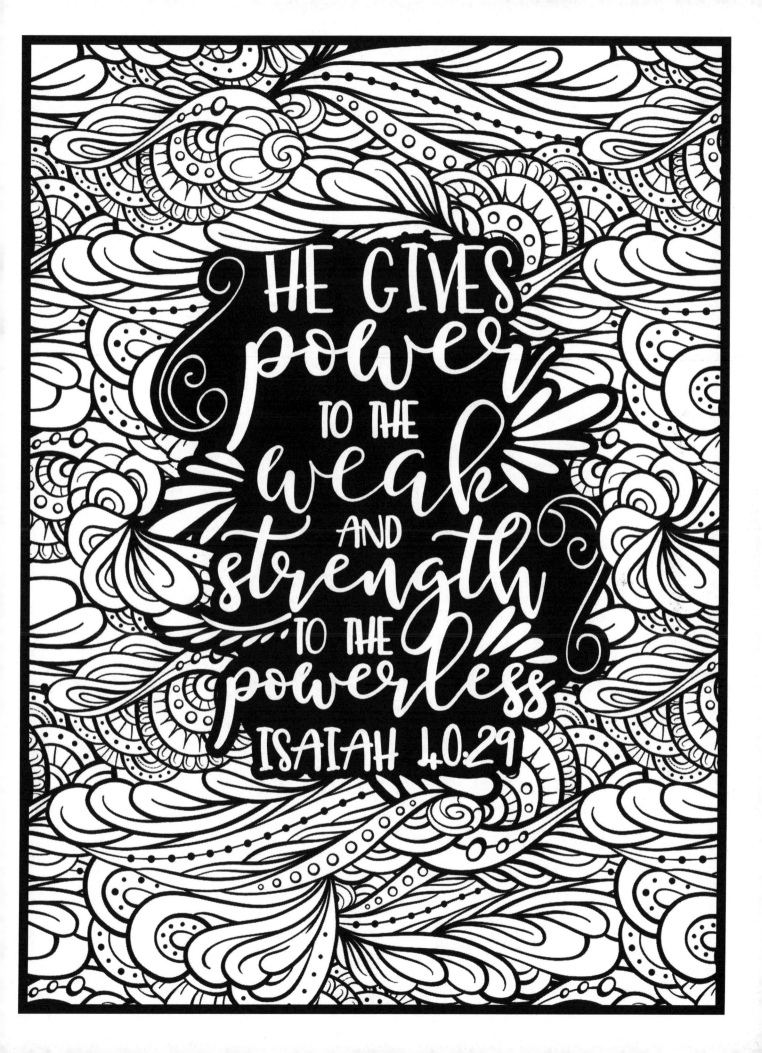

For now we see indistinctly, as in a mirror, but then face to face. Now I know in part, but then I will know fully, as I am fully known. Now these three remain: faith, hope, and love. But the greatest of these is love.

1 Corinthians 13:12-13 (HCSB)

Therefore, that I might not become too elated, a thorn in the flesh was given to me, an angel of Satan, to beat me, to keep me from being too elated. Three times I begged the Lord about this, that it might leave me, but he said to me, "My grace is sufficient for you, for power is made perfect in weakness." I will rather boast most gladly of my weaknesses, in order that the power of Christ may dwell with me.

2 Corinthians 12:7-9 (NABRE)

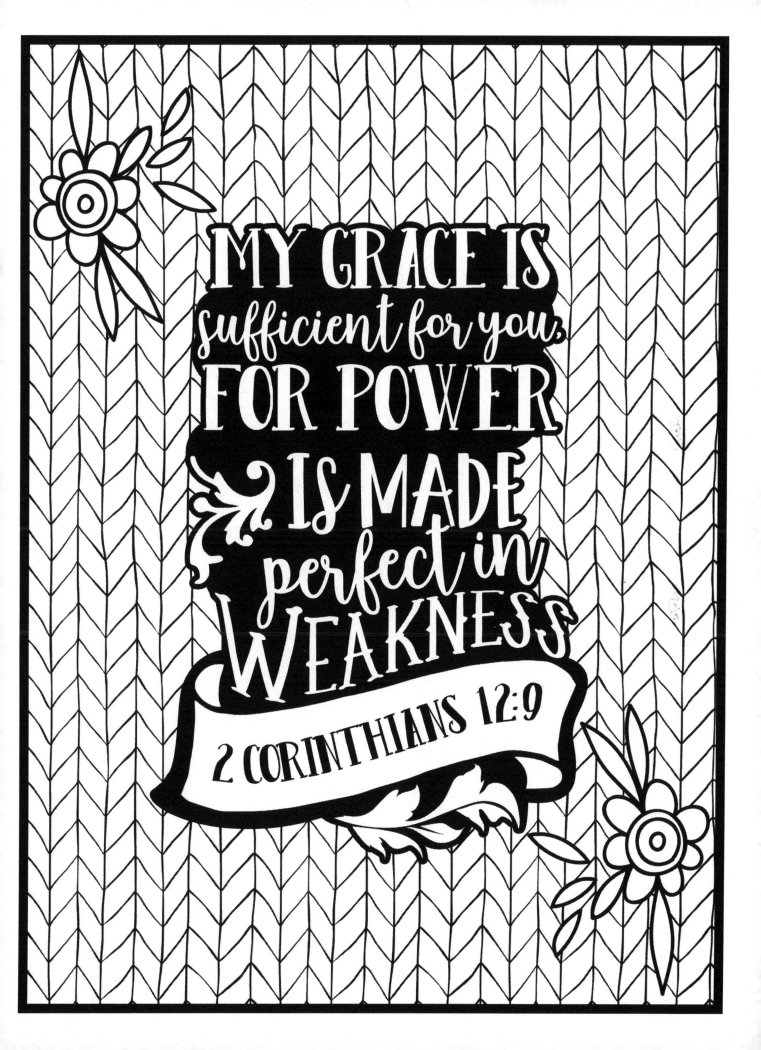

Let love be genuine; hate what is evil, hold fast to what is good; love one another with mutual affection; outdo one another in showing honor. Do not lag in zeal, be ardent in spirit, serve the Lord. Rejoice in hope, be patient in suffering, persevere in prayer. Contribute to the needs of the saints; extend hospitality to strangers.

Romans 12:9-13 (NRSV)

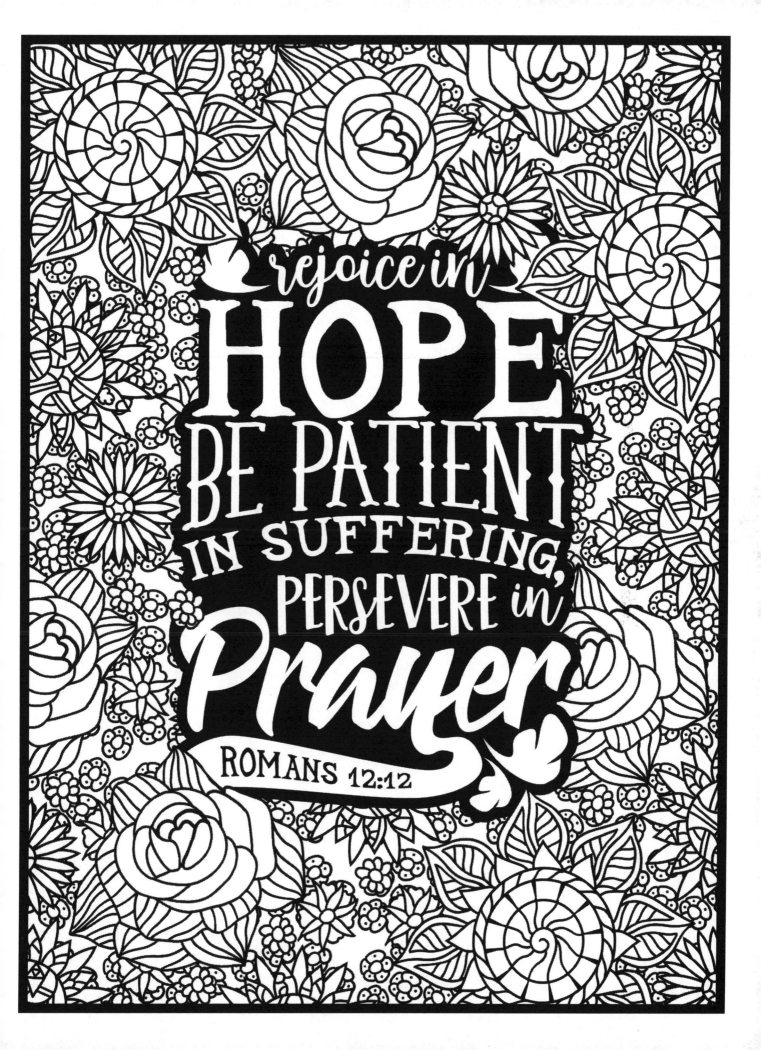

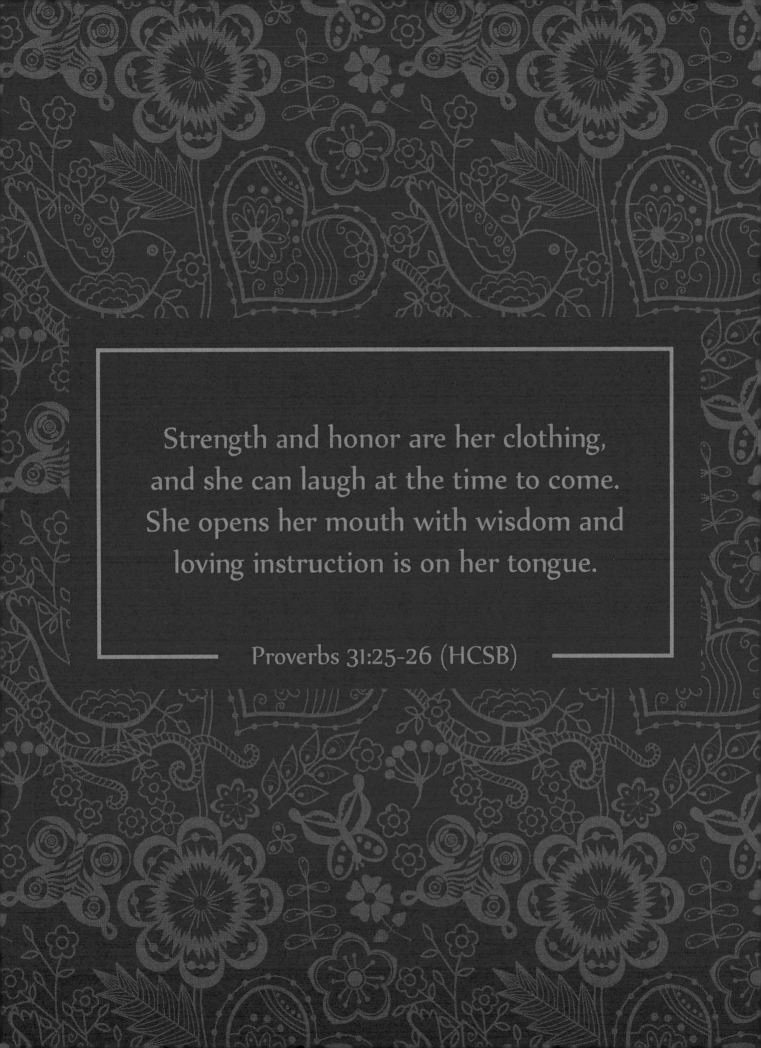

Strength and honor are her clothing,
and she can laugh at the time to come.
She opens her mouth with wisdom and
loving instruction is on her tongue.

Proverbs 31:25-26 (HCSB)

She opens her mouth with wisdom and loving instruction is on her tongue.

PROVERBS 31:26

When they arrived, Samuel saw Eliab and thought, "Surely the Lord's anointed stands here before the Lord." But the Lord said to Samuel, "Do not consider his appearance or his height, for I have rejected him. The Lord does not look at the things human beings look at. People look at the outward appearance, but the Lord looks at the heart."

1 Samuel 16:6-7 (NIV)

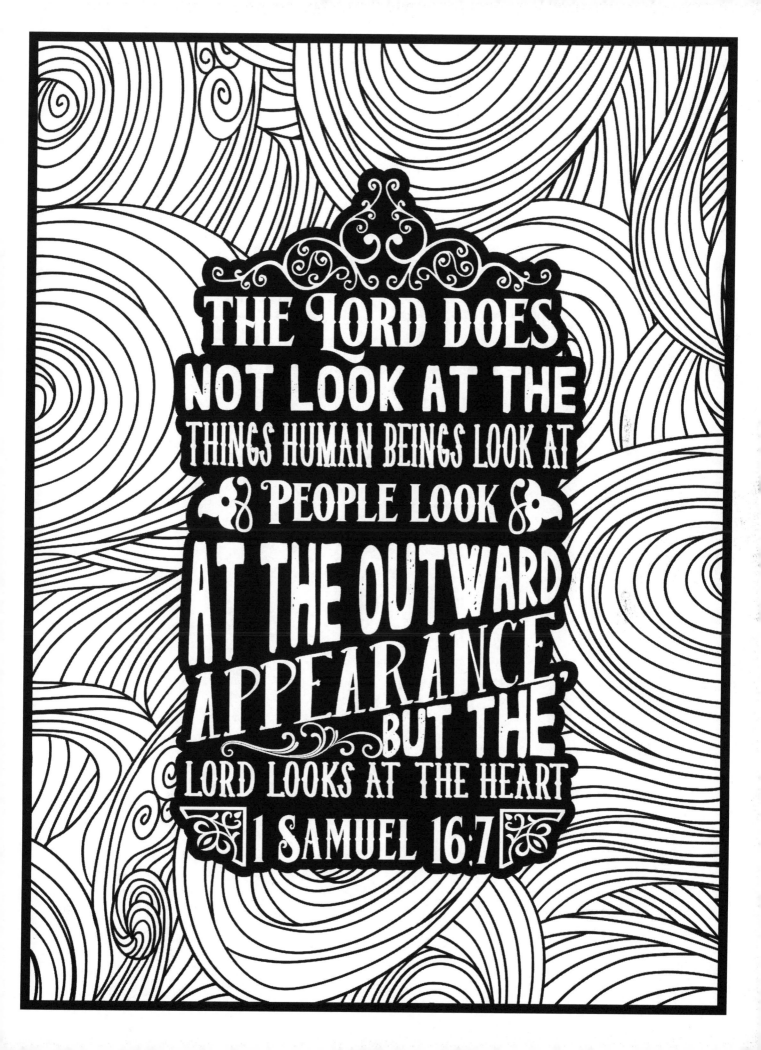

Our soul waits for the Lord, he is our help and shield. For in him our hearts rejoice; in his holy name we trust. May your mercy, Lord, be upon us; as we put our hope in you.

Psalm 33:20-22 (NABRE)

Dear friends, let us love one another, for love comes from God. Everyone who loves has been born of God and knows God. Whoever does not love does not know God, because God is love. This is how God showed his love among us: He sent his one and only Son into the world that we might live through him.

1 John 4:7-9 (NIV)

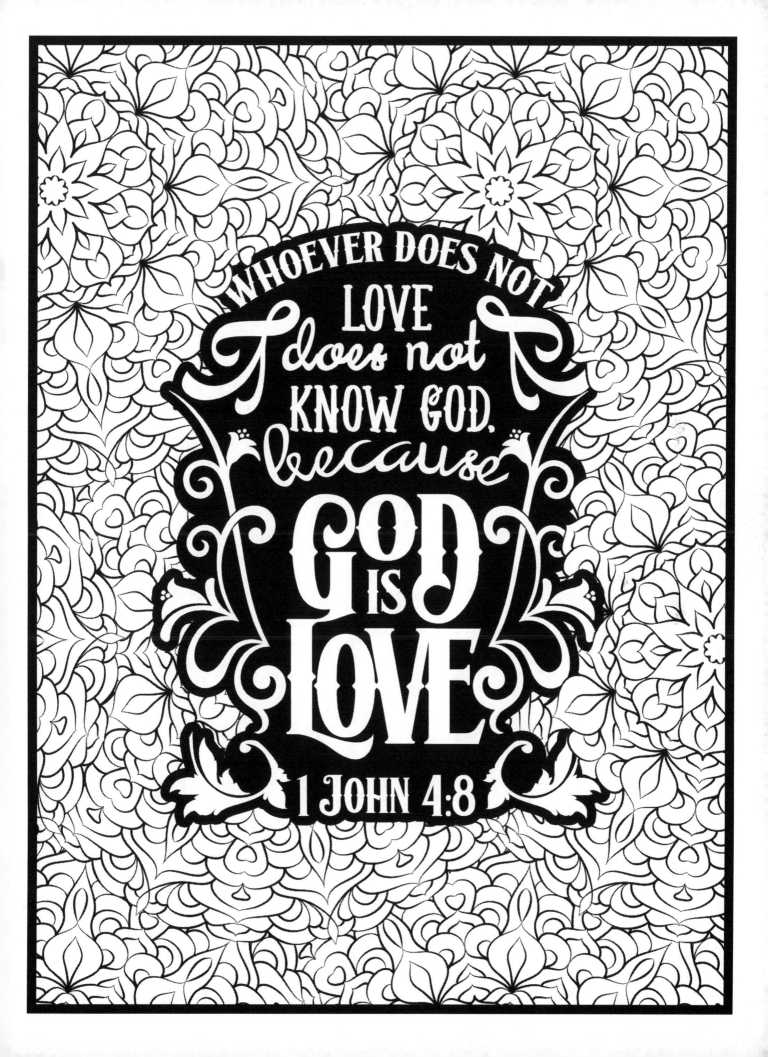

Whom have I in heaven but you? And there is nothing on earth that I desire other than you. My flesh and my heart may fail, but God is the strength of my heart and my portion forever.

— Psalm 73:25-26 (NRSV) —

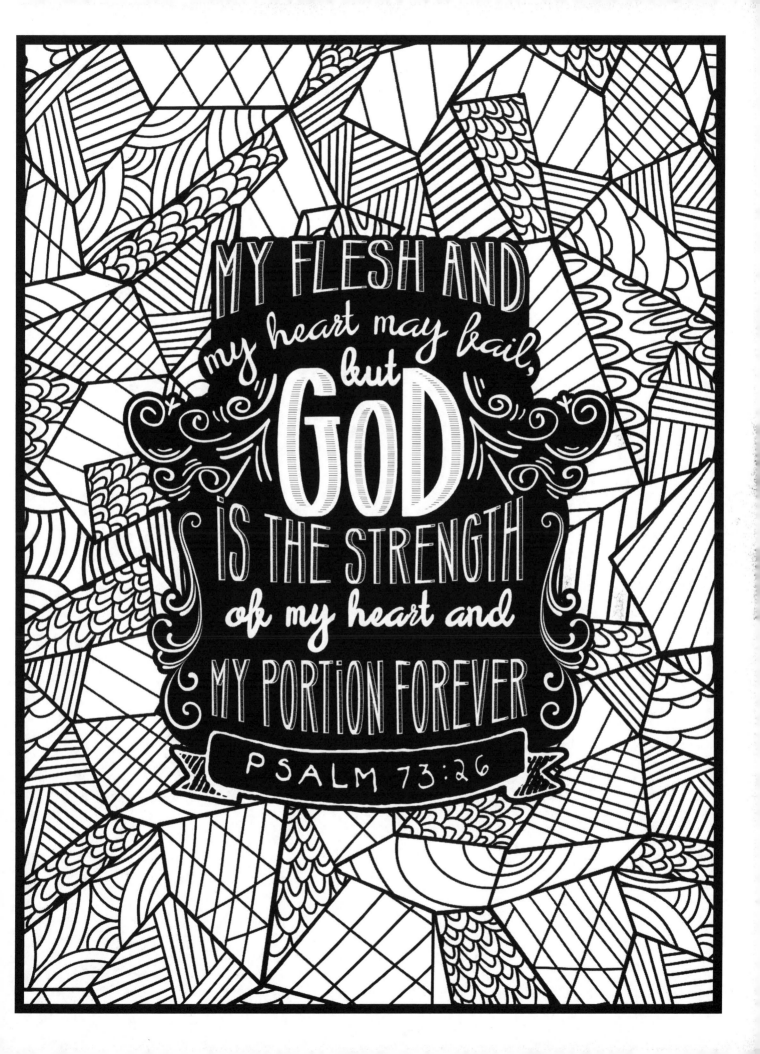

Blessed are those who hunger and thirst for righteousness, for they shall be filled. Blessed are the merciful, for they shall obtain mercy. Blessed are the pure in heart, for they shall see God.

Matthew 5:6-8 (NKJV)

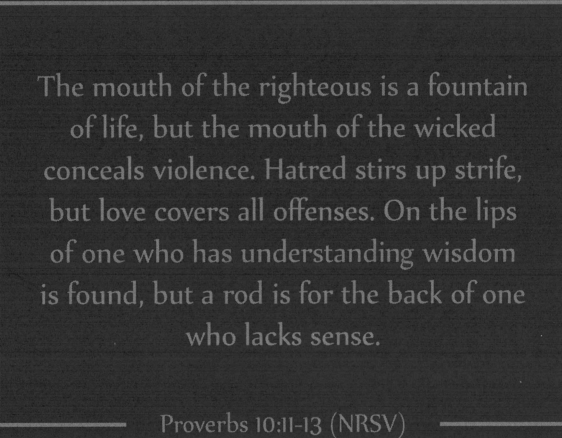

The mouth of the righteous is a fountain of life, but the mouth of the wicked conceals violence. Hatred stirs up strife, but love covers all offenses. On the lips of one who has understanding wisdom is found, but a rod is for the back of one who lacks sense.

Proverbs 10:11-13 (NRSV)

I will never forget this awful time, as I grieve over my loss. Yet I still dare to hope when I remember this: The faithful love of the Lord never ends! His mercies never cease. Great is his faithfulness; his mercies begin afresh each morning. I say to myself, "The Lord is my inheritance; therefore, I will hope in him!"

Lamentations 3:20-24 (NLT)

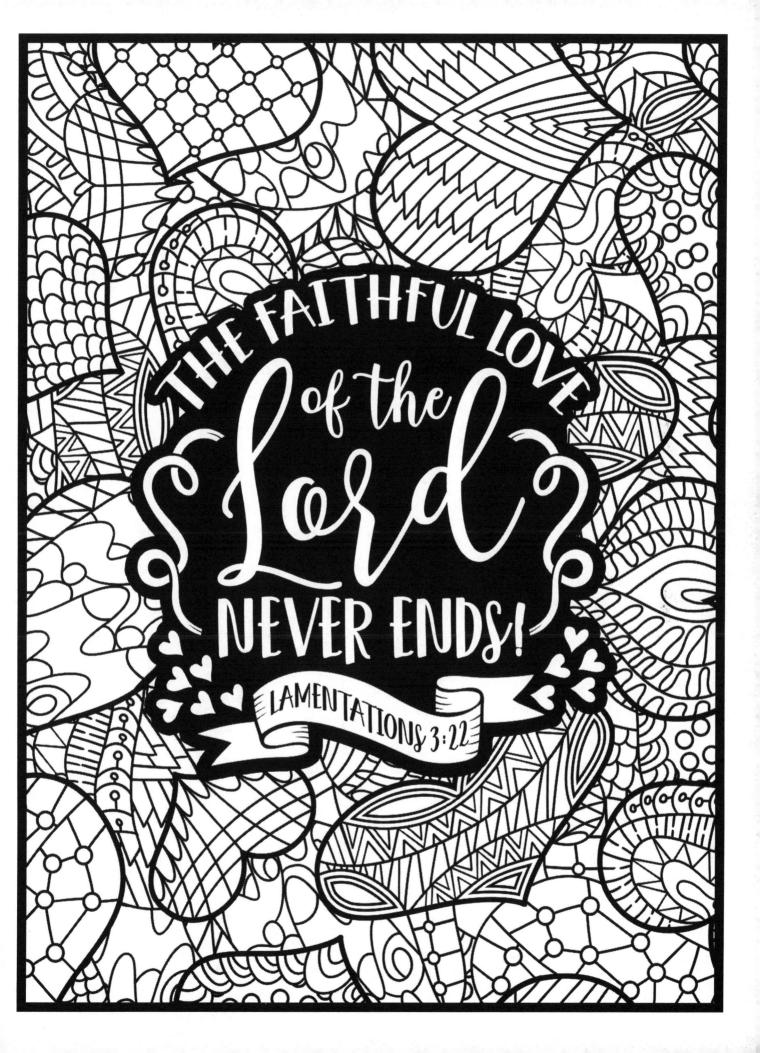

Her sons rise up and call her blessed. Her husband also praises her: "Many women are capable, but you surpass them all!" Charm is deceptive and beauty is fleeting, but a woman who fears the Lord will be praised.

Proverbs 31:28-30 (HCSB)

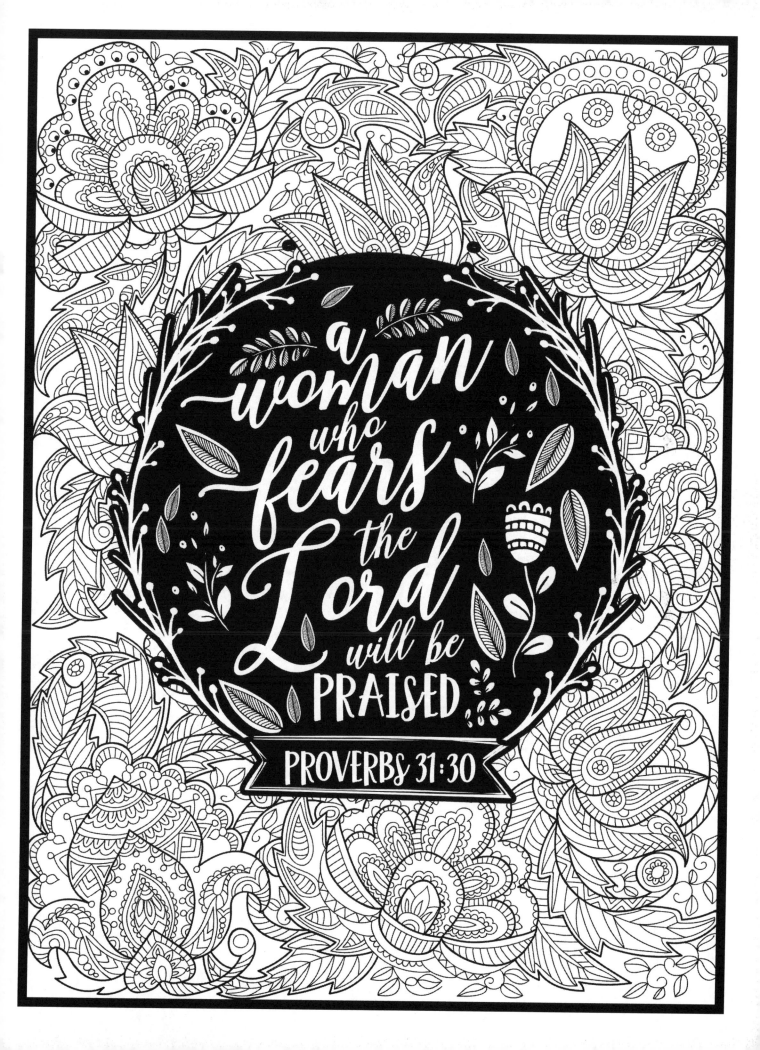

If I speak human or angelic languages but do not have love, I am a sounding gong or a clanging cymbal. If I have the gift of prophecy and understand all mysteries and all knowledge, and if I have all faith so that I can move mountains but do not have love, I am nothing. And if I donate all my goods to feed the poor, and if I give my body in order to boast but do not have love, I gain nothing.

1 Corinthians 13:1-3 (HCSB)

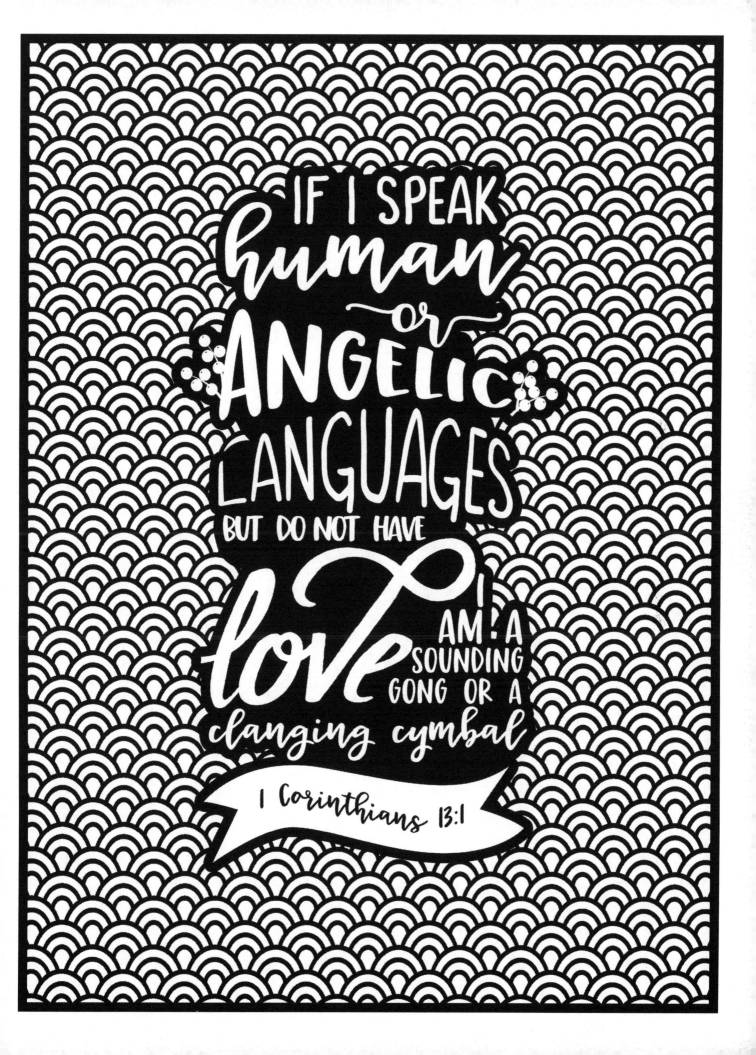

Like a scarlet strand, your lips, and your mouth – lovely! Like pomegranate halves, your cheeks behind your veil. Like a tower of David, your neck, built in courses, a thousand shields hanging upon it, all the armor of warriors.

Song of Solomon 4:3-4 (NABRE)

All scripture is inspired by God and is useful for teaching, for refutation, for correction, and for training in righteousness, so that one who belongs to God may be competent, equipped for every good work.

2 Timothy 3:16-17 (NABRE)

Finally, draw your strength from the Lord and from his mighty power. Put on the armor of God so that you may be able to stand firm against the tactics of the devil. For our struggle is not with flesh and blood but with the principalities, with the powers, with the world rulers of this present darkness, with the evil spirits in the heavens.

Ephesians 6:10-12 (NABRE)

On that day, you will say: I give you thanks, O Lord; though you have been angry with me, your anger has abated, and you have consoled me. God indeed is my salvation; I am confident and unafraid. For the Lord is my strength and my might, and he has been my salvation.

Isaiah 12:1-2 (NABRE)

Let the word of Christ dwell in you richly, as in all wisdom you teach and admonish one another, singing psalms, hymns, and spiritual songs with gratitude in your hearts to God. And whatever you do, in word or in deed, do everything in the name of the Lord Jesus, giving thanks to God the Father through him.

Colossians 3:16-17 (NABRE)

Hear, O Israel! The Lord is our God, the Lord alone! Therefore, you shall love the Lord, your God, with your whole heart, and with your whole being, and with your whole strength. Take to heart these words which I command you today. Keep repeating them to your children. Recite them when you are at home and when you are away, when you lie down and when you get up.

Deuteronomy 6:4-7 (NABRE)

Get rid of all bitterness, rage and anger, brawling and slander, along with every form of malice. Be kind and compassionate to one another, forgiving each other, just as in Christ God forgave you.

Ephesians 4:31-32 (NIV)

Praise the Lord! How joyful are those who fear the Lord and delight in obeying his commands. Their children will be successful everywhere; an entire generation of godly people will be blessed. They themselves will be wealthy, and their good deeds will last forever. Light shines in the darkness for the godly. They are generous, compassionate, and righteous.

Psalm 112:1-4 (NLT)

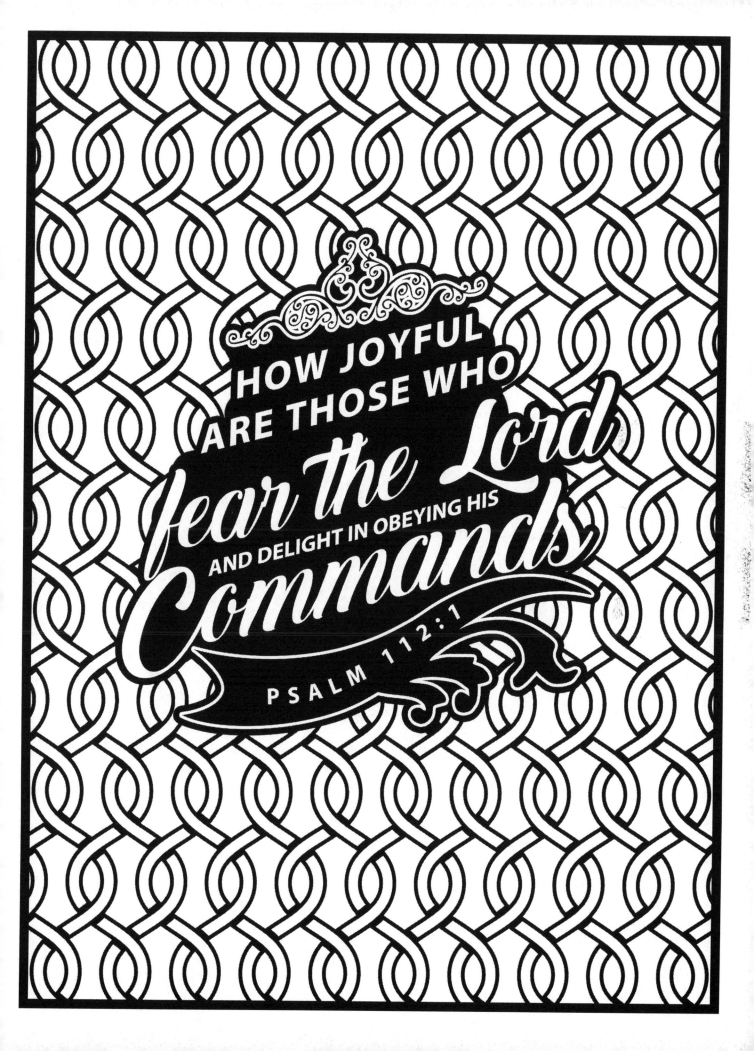

For you are saved by grace through faith, and this is not from yourselves; it is God's gift – not from works, so that no one can boast. For we are his creation, created in Christ Jesus for good works, which God prepared ahead of time so that we should walk in them.

Ephesians 2:8-10 (HCSB)

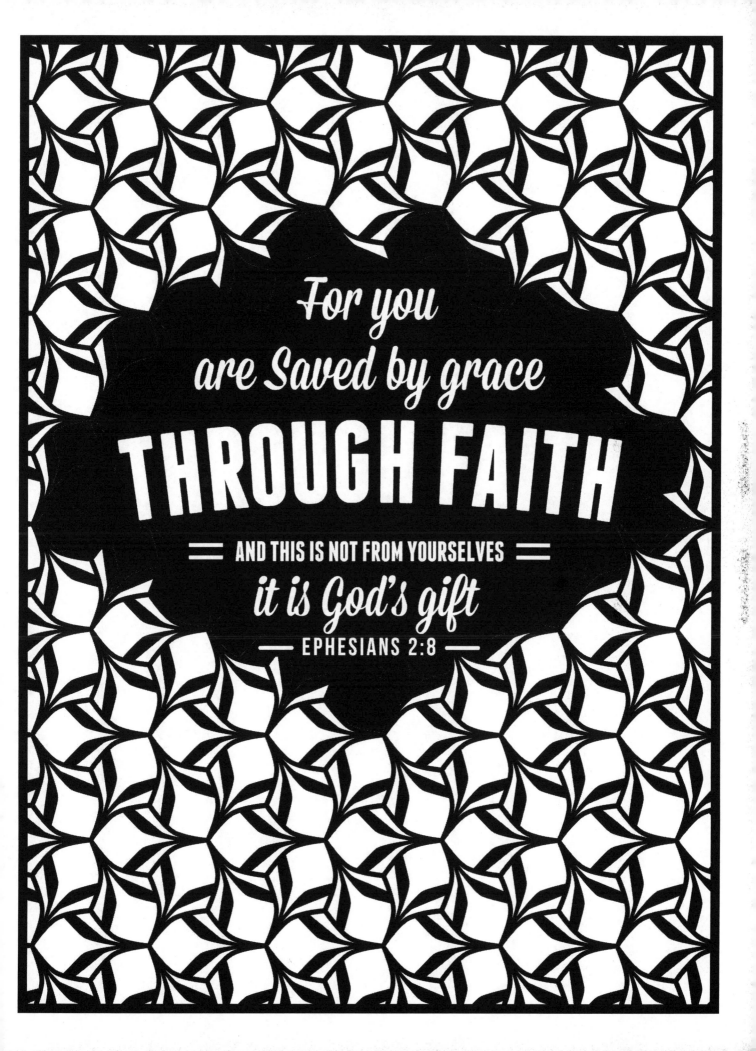

But the Holy Spirit produces this
kind of fruit in our lives: love, joy,
peace, patience, kindness, goodness,
faithfulness, gentleness, and self-control.
There is no law against these things!

Galatians 5:22-23 (NLT)

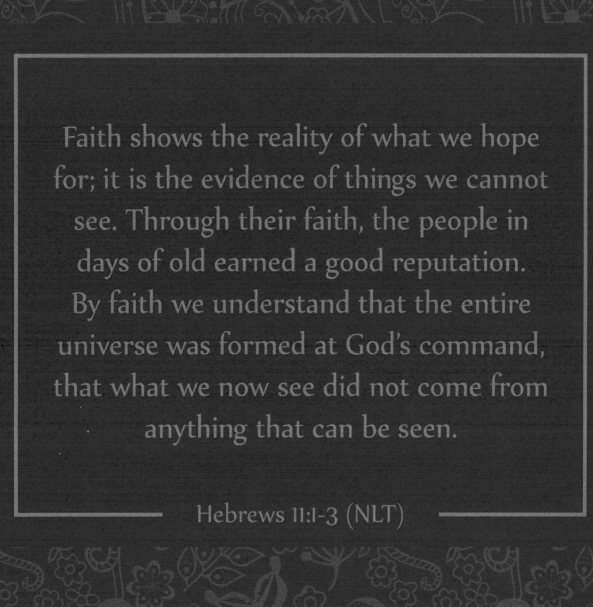

Faith shows the reality of what we hope for; it is the evidence of things we cannot see. Through their faith, the people in days of old earned a good reputation. By faith we understand that the entire universe was formed at God's command, that what we now see did not come from anything that can be seen.

Hebrews 11:1-3 (NLT)

Are any among you suffering? They should pray. Are any cheerful? They should sing songs of praise. Are any among you sick? They should call for the elders of the church and have them pray over them, anointing them with oil in the name of the Lord. The prayer of faith will save the sick, and the Lord will raise them up; and anyone who has committed sins will be forgiven.

James 5:13-15 (NRSV)

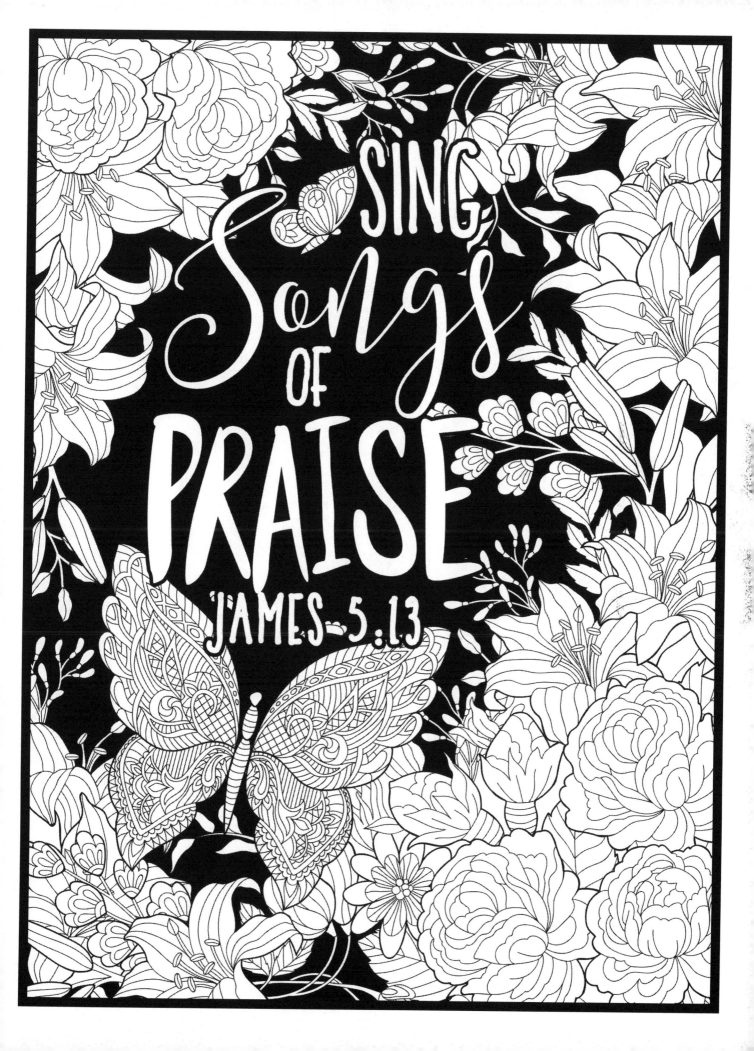

There are different kinds of spiritual gifts, but the same Spirit is the source of them all. There are different kinds of service, but we serve the same Lord. God works in different ways, but it is the same God who does the work in all of us.

1 Corinthians 4-6 (NLT)

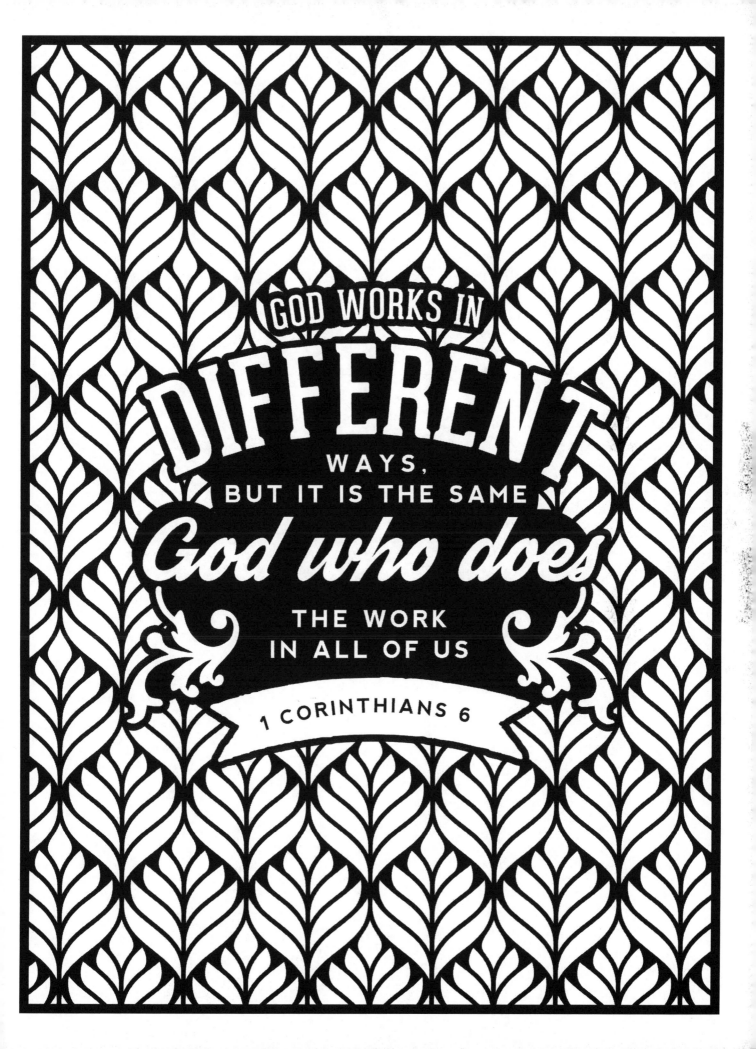

BE SURE TO FOLLOW US
ON SOCIAL MEDIA
FOR THE LATEST NEWS,
SNEAK PEEKS, & GIVEAWAYS

inspiredtograce

Inspired-to-Grace

@inspired2grace

ADD YOURSELF TO OUR
MONTHLY NEWSLETTER FOR FREE DIGITAL
DOWNLOADS AND DISCOUNT CODES
www.inspiredtograce.com/newsletter

CHECK OUT OUR OTHER BOOKS!

WWW.INSPIREDTOGRACE.COM

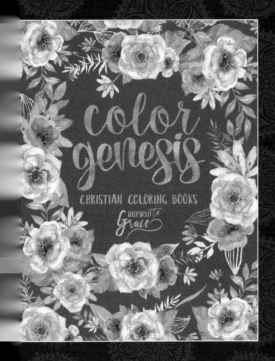

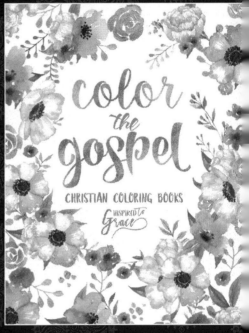

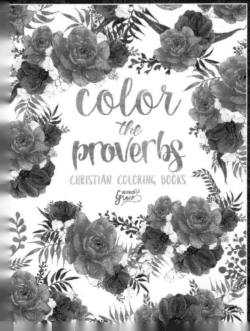

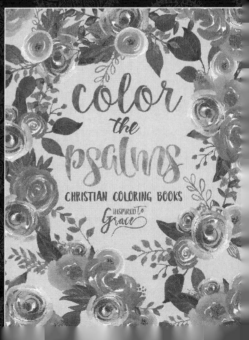

CHECK OUT OUR OTHER BOOKS!

WWW.INSPIREDTOGRACE.COM

   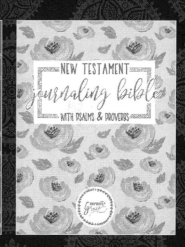

CHRISTIAN PLANNER *twenty seventeen* WEEKLY PRAYER JOURNAL

CHRISTIAN PLANNER *twenty seventeen* WEEKLY PRAYER JOURNAL

NEW TESTAMENT *journaling bible* WITH PSALMS & PROVERBS

  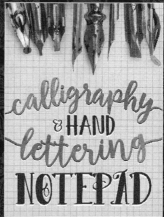

Verses FOR Men — Grace — LARGE PRINT EDITION

verses for women A CHRISTIAN COLORING BOOK

calligraphy & HAND *lettering* NOTEPAD

INSPIRED to grace 6-MONTH BIBLE STUDY JOURNAL COLORING EDITION

INSPIRED to grace 6-MONTH PRAYER JOURNAL COLORING EDITION

joy to the world A CHRISTIAN COLOURING BOOK

CHECK OUT OUR OTHER BOOKS!

WWW.INSPIREDTOGRACE.COM

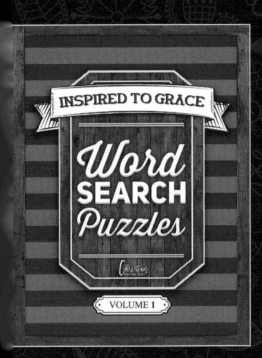

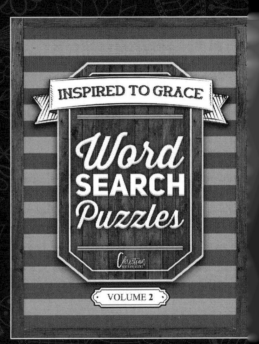

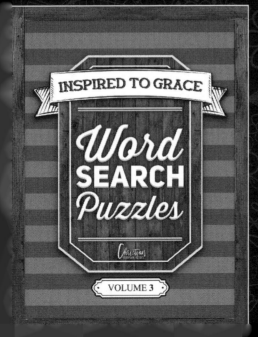

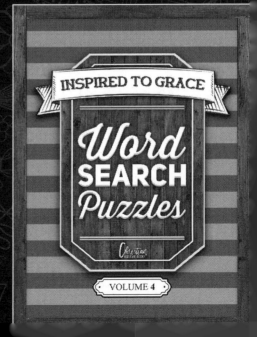

Made in the USA
Columbia, SC
16 August 2018